Thank y

You can personalize this book for your sister!

Find a special photograph of you!
Simply tape your photo on the corners and place over the photo on this page.
Make sure that your photo shows through the window of the book's front cover.

Thank You
Sister

It is not what you have in your life that counts
but who you have in your life that counts.

RITA FIESEL

Thank You Sister

A Keepsake in Celebration of Sisters

Brentwood, Tennessee

Thank You, Sister

Copyright © 2004 GRQ, Inc.

ISBN 1-59475-048-3

Published by Blue Sky Ink

Brentwood, Tennessee.

Editor: Lila Empson

Writer: Phillip H. Barnhart

Cover and text design: Diane Whisner

04 05 06   4 3 2 1

A sister is dear to you always,
for she is someone who
is always a part
of all the favorite memories
that you keep very close to
your heart.

AUTHOR UNKNOWN

How very good and pleasant it is
when kindred live together in unity!

PSALM 133:1 NRSV

Introduction

*D*ear sister, you are a gift from God to me, and I am grateful for our relationship over the years. When we were kids I thought we were close, but we're even closer now. Then we giggled and whispered secrets and wore each other's clothes. Now we talk on the phone and share recipes and visit each other on holidays.

When either one of us has a crisis, the other one is knocking on the door. When either has an achievement or accomplishment, the other is there leading cheers. I think of how your strengths have become mine, mine yours, and how each of us is better because of the other.

Dear sister, I love you.

Anyone who does the will of my
Father in heaven is my brother
and sister and mother!

MATTHEW 12:50 NLT

*A sister is someone who
will quietly listen when
you just want to talk for
a while.*

AUTHOR UNKNOWN

*The best thing about having a sister is
that I always had a friend.*

CALI RAE TURNER

*How do people make it through
life without a sister?*

SARA CORPENING

There can be no situation
in which the conversation
of my dear sister will
not administer some
comfort to me.

MARY MONTAGU

*Live out your God-created identity. Live
generously and graciously toward others,
the way God lives toward you.*

MATTHEW 5:48 THE MESSAGE

The mildest, drowsiest sister has been known to turn tiger if her sibling is in trouble.

CLARA ORTEGA

Sweet is the voice of a sister in the season of sorrow.

BENJAMIN DISRAELI

One Sister Remembers...

Since there were ten people in our family, my sisters and I did the dishes every night. Because it took so long, we spent the time singing. To this day, if there are two or more of us in a kitchen, we sing.

Because of such a big family, Dad was always looking for ways to earn extra money. Hearing us singing in the kitchen, he got an idea. He started taking us to all the surrounding fairs where they had talent contests. Sometimes first prize was as much as fifty dollars. He'd take however many of us girls were available at the time. We won a lot of contests.

With the money, Dad bought things we needed. And some we didn't.

Those who sow righteousness get a true reward.

PROVERBS 11:18 NRSV

*More than Santa Claus, your sister
knows when you've been bad and good.*

LINDA SUNSHINE

Whatever you do, they will love you; even if they don't love you they are connected to you till you die. You can be boring and tedious with sisters, whereas you have to put on a good face with friends.

<small>Deborah Moggach</small>

*A sister can be seen as someone who is both ourselves
and very much not ourselves—a special kind of double.*

TONI MORRISON

*What's the good of news if you haven't
a sister to share it with?*

JENNY DEVRIES

Two are better than one. . . .
for if they fall, one will lift
up the other.

ECCLESIASTES 4:9–10 NRSV

In thee my soul shall own combined the sister and the friend.

CATHERINE KILLIGREW

19

*May the LORD keep watch between you and
me when we are away from each other.*

GENESIS 31:49 NIV

*The LORD has done great things for us,
and we are filled with joy.*

PSALM 126:3 NIV

*Sisters share the scent
and smells, the feel of a
common childhood.*

PAM BROWN

A sister smiles when one tells one's stories—for she knows where the decoration has been added.

CHRIS MONTAIGNE

Did You Know?

Did you know there is a town in the United States called Sisters? It's in Oregon and has a population of 919. It is set among towering forests of Ponderosa pines, the snowy Cascade mountains, pristine rivers, lakes and streams, sun-drenched days, and star-filled nights. The town of Sisters was named for the Three Sisters mountains nearby. Some say the mountains were originally named Faith, Hope, and Charity by early pioneers but came to be called Three Sisters because they were so close together.

May the Lord continually bless you with heaven's blessings as well as with human joys.

PSALM 128:5 TLB

*What we have once
enjoyed we can never lose.
All that we love deeply
becomes a part of us.*

HELEN KELLER

*If your sister is in a tearing hurry to go
out and cannot catch your eye, she's
wearing your best sweater.*

PAM BROWN

*When sisters stand shoulder to shoulder,
who stands a chance against us?*

PAM BROWN

Recall it as often as you wish, a happy memory never wears out.

LIBBIE FUDIM

*If you don't understand how a
woman could both love her sister
dearly and want to wring her neck
at the same time, then you were
probably an only child.*

LINDA SUNSHINE

*People are motivated more by love
and joy than anything else.*

HENRY H. MITCHELL

*Some people make the world
special just by being in it.*

ROBERT NOTTING

*Only the heart speaks to the heart. I need to tell you
my story and I need to hear yours, so that we may
share our secrets and trust our hearts.*

JUDY COLLINS

Survival Tip

Remember, a Sister Is:

1. One of the best gifts you get.

2. Someone to laugh with.

3. Someone to share with.

4. Someone you can't fool for long.

5. A fellow conspirator.

6. Someone to tell your stories to.

7. Someone to practice your ideas on.

8. Someone who comes with the territory.

9. Someone who takes your side.

10. A good friend.

*Pleasant words are a
honeycomb, sweet to the
soul and healing to
the bones.*

PROVERBS 16:24 NIV

Don't cry because it's over; smile because it happened.

Author Unknown

*Sisters function as a safety net in a chaotic
world simply by being there for each other.*

CAROL SALINE

*Sister is probably the most competitive
relationship within the family, but once the
sisters are grown, it becomes the strongest one.*

MARGARET MEAD

There are no cookie cutters in heaven. With his hand he's shaped every one.

JOHN POWERS

You have a unique message to deliver, a unique song to sing, a unique act of love to bestow. This message, this song, and this act of love have been entrusted exclusively to the one and only you.

JOHN POWELL

A Sister Takes One

Bonnie was one of five girls in her family, all of them about two years apart. When she was seven, all the girls came down with whooping cough and their mother sent for the doctor to give them shots. Bonnie hated shots and made a deal with her sister, Susan. If Susan would take Bonnie's shot for her, she could play with her new doll for a week.

The doctor lined up the girls, and Susan went first. Bonnie hid out behind the house, and Susan went to the back of the line and got a second shot. The doctor knew only that the right number of shots had been given.

Bonnie still thinks of Susan as the sister who "took one" for her.

Be kind to one another,
tenderhearted, forgiving
one another, as God in
Christ has forgiven you.

EPHESIANS 4:32 NRSV

*We learn to love before
we learn anything else.*

AUTHOR UNKNOWN

We are sisters. We will always be sisters.
Our differences may never go away, but
neither will our song.

ELIZABETH FISHEL

To have a loving relationship with a sister
is to have a soul mate for life.

VICTORIA SECUNDA

*Don't allow the clock
and the calendar to
blind you to the fact
that each moment of
your life is a miracle
and a mystery.*

H. G. WELLS

Love one another the way I loved you.
This is the very best way to love.
Put your life on the line for your friends.

JOHN 15:12–13 THE MESSAGE

Love can only be done with verbs.

CARLYLE MARNEY

Everything I understand,
I understand only because I love.

LEO TOLSTOY

One Sister Remembers . . .

I remember when Mom and Dad saved until they had enough money to buy a larger house, and we drove across town to see it. My sister, Dianne, and I ran into the house and quickly went upstairs. Now we would finally have separate bedrooms.

The next week, my sister and I got set up in our separate rooms. This is going to be great, we both said. No more sharing a bed. No more cramming clothes into a closet. But after four days in separate rooms, Dianne and I were so lonely we didn't know what to do. We begged Mom and Dad to let us have the same room. They did, and Mom made the extra one into an office for Dad.

We know that just as you share in our sufferings,
so also you share in our comfort.

2 Corinthians 1:7 niv

Sisters touch your heart in ways no other
could. Sisters share their hopes, fears,
love, everything they have.

Carrie Bagwell

*Love cannot be measured in a
lab or proved in a textbook.
Yet it, and it alone, is the
substance of all things visible.
Without love, there can be no
creativity. Without creativity,
there can be no life.*

AUTHOR UNKNOWN

*It may go without saying
but it should not go unsaid.*

PAUL SELZMAN

I am here to live out loud.

ÉMILE ZOLA

Each time I think of you,
I give thanks to my God.

PHILIPPIANS 1:3 NLT

*Love is discovery
without end.*

EARNEST LARSEN

Have unity of spirit, sympathy,
love for one another.

1 PETER 3:8 NRSV

Follow the way of love.

1 CORINTHIANS 14:1 NIV

We are all in one small boat
on a stormy sea, and we owe
each other a terrible loyalty.

G. K. CHESTERTON

Sisterly love is, of all sentiments,
the most abstract. Nature does
not grant it any functions.

UGO BETTI

Did You Know?

Did you know the Lennon Sisters made their debut appearance on the *Lawrence Welk Show* on Christmas Eve in 1955? The sisters—Dianne, Peggy, Kathy, and Janet—became an overnight sensation and one of television's most popular musical acts. The Lennon Sisters recorded many albums, and received a star on the Hollywood Hall of Fame in 1987.

When asked why their voices blended so well, one of them said, "We're sisters, aren't we?"

*When we love each
other God lives in us.*

1 John 4:12 tlb

*You can go back and
have what you like if you
remember it well enough.*

RICHARD LLEWELLYN

To the outside world we grow old.
But not to sisters.

CLARA ORTEGA

If God had a wallet, your
picture would be in it.

AUTHOR UNKNOWN

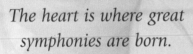

*The heart is where great
symphonies are born.*

CALVIN MILLER

As the pressures of life intensify,
sometimes the difference
between going after a dream
and remaining passive is
having some say,
"I believe in you!"

GARY SMALLEY

Happiness is not a station you arrive at,
but a manner of traveling.

CECIL MURPHEY

If you really want to be happy,
nobody can stop you.

SISTER MARY TRICKY

Wherever we find ourselves, there is always a unique constellation of passion and action to embrace or reject. In every moment and at every place, we confront inordinate possibilities for coming alive in significant action.

DAVID O. WOODYARD

Survival Tips

Pointers for Sisters:

1. Say "I love you" often.

2. Verbalize annoyances.

3. When you have something to say, say it.

4. Let your inside out.

5. Be active in your love.

6. Reveal what you feel.

7. Put on a happy face.

8. Talk it over.

9. Act better than you feel.

10. Make the trip from your head to your heart.

Whatever is good and
perfect comes to us
from God.

JAMES 1:17 TLB

Money can buy you a wonderful dog, but only love will make him wag his tail.

AUTHOR UNKNOWN

Be humble, for you are made of earth.
Be noble, for you are made of stars.

Serbian Proverb

Humor is laughing at what you haven't
got when you ought to have it.

Langston Hughes

It is requisite for the relaxation of the mind that we make use, from time to time, of playful deeds and jokes.

SAINT THOMAS AQUINAS

You and I were created for joy.

Lewis B. Smedes

Teammates Always

Many people thought Jackie and Becky were twins, but they were about thirteen months apart. Growing up, they had the usual squabbles sisters have, but on the basketball court they were always hand and glove. From the time they played together on their driveway to when they led their high-school team to a city championship, Jackie and Becky were teammates who perfectly anticipated each other's moves. In fact, as they got older, one hardly did anything without the other.

They were roommates in college, started their teaching careers in the same school, and recently had a double wedding in their childhood church. "Teammates always," they said to each other as they walked down the aisle.

I do not cease to give thanks
for you as I remember you
in my prayers.

EPHESIANS 1:16 NRSV

*To be trusted is a
greater compliment
than to be loved.*

GEORGE MACDONALD

The privilege of a lifetime
is being who you are.

AUTHOR UNKNOWN

Whatever you do in terms of telling a story,
the most important thing you can
do is define who you are.

JOHN PATRICK SHANLEY

*The heart that loves
is always young.*

GREEK PROVERB

*Only love can be divided endlessly
and still not diminish.*

ANNE MORROW LINDBERGH

*Perfect love means to love the one through
whom one becomes unhappy.*

SÖREN KIERKEGAARD

*Don't worry about any-
thing; instead, pray about
everything. Tell God what
you need, and thank him
for all he has done.*

PHILIPPIANS 4:6 NLT

One Sister Remembers...

My sister Penny married younger than I did and had four children by the time I had one. It was expensive raising four little children: clothes and food to buy, rent to pay on a big house, braces for crooked teeth.

My sister worked hard to take care of her children. When they were small, she always had two jobs. One time she had three. For nearly four years, she sold merchandise door to door—books, mops, and cookware, among other things. After her kids were in school, she drove a school bus. At some point during that time, she sold cosmetics to her friends.

There wasn't anything my sister wouldn't do for her children.

*The Holy Spirit will teach you in that very
hour what you ought to say.*

LUKE 12:12 NASB

*The best way to light up the world
is with a current of love.*

AUTHOR UNKNOWN

*Words are inadequate, we say.
So they often are. But they are
nonetheless precious. A word fitly
spoken is like "apples of gold in
pictures of silver." In a time of crisis
we learn how intensely we need both
flesh and the word. We cannot do
well without either one. The bodily
presence of people we love is greatly
comforting, and their silent
companionship blesses us.*

ELISABETH ELLIOT

Love isn't what makes the world go around.
It is what makes the ride worthwhile.

Franklin P. Jones

Love is faith internalized and hope actualized.

Robert T. Young

Before they call I will answer;
while they are still speaking
I will hear.

ISAIAH 65:24 NIV

*One's sister is a part of
one's essential self, an
eternal presence of
one's heart and soul
and memory.*

S<small>USAN</small> C<small>ABILL</small>

Because of your unfailing love,
I can enter your house.

PSALM 5:7 NLT

My purpose is that they may be encouraged
in heart and united in love.

COLOSSIANS 2:2 NIV

Chance made us sisters;
heart made us friends.

AUTHOR UNKNOWN

*Is solace anywhere more
comforting than that in
the arms of a sister?*

ALICE WALKER

Did You Know?

Did you know the famous Pointer Sisters honed their singing technique at the West Oakland Church of God in Oakland, California, where their father was pastor? Nominated for a Grammy ten times and winning that honor three times in widely varied categories, it all began when they sang together in church. Ruth, Anita, and June were sisters whose faith led them to a deep and lasting bond with one another.

*He who began a good work
in you will perfect it until
the day of Christ Jesus.*

PHILIPPIANS 1:6 NASB

*There is no substitute for
the comfort supplied by
the utterly taken-for-granted
relationship.*

IRIS MURDOCH

*Each of our lives will always
be a special part of the other.*

AUTHOR UNKNOWN

*Like branches on a tree we grow in different
directions, yet our roots remain as one.*

AUTHOR UNKNOWN

My sister is in my heart.
She opens doors to rooms
I never knew were there,
breaks through walls I
don't recall building.

LISA LORDEN

Our Lord gave us his love generously not in order that we might be loved, but that we might be freed to love one another.

REUEL L. HOWE

*A sister is someone to laugh with and share with,
to work with, and join in the fun.*

AUTHOR UNKNOWN

*Helping one another is part of the
religion of sisterhood.*

LOUISA MAY ALCOTT

We were glad we could talk about these things. Often such experiences remain hidden and cause much shame and guilt. But by confessing to each other how easily we are seduced by the attractions of the world, we affirmed our true commitment and safeguarded that commitment in each other.

HENRI J. M. NOUWEN

Survival Tips

Truths for Sisters:

1. Your sister is a blessing.

2. Compassion wins the day.

3. Love leaves its arithmetic at home.

4. You can be wrong.

5. You can come in second.

6. Hearing is more than listening.

7. Communicating is more than talking.

8. You teach each other.

9. Learn to negotiate.

10. A problem shared is half the burden.

11. A joy shared is twice the blessing.

12. You are for each other.

*We have this treasure in jars
of clay to show that this
all-surpassing power is
from God.*

2 CORINTHIANS 4:7 NIV

Not everything that counts can be counted.

AUTHOR UNKNOWN

When I work hardest on self-improvement,
my relationships with others improve.

GRETCHEN BEAUBIER

To the world you might be one person, but to one person you might be the world.

AUTHOR UNKNOWN

Life is too short to stuff a mushroom.

SHIRLEY CONRAN

*The proverb makers remind us that part of the
sound one hears in a seashell is created by the
pulse and throb of the hand holding it.*

FRED CRADDOCK

One Big Offering

Tiffie is seven, Sandie is five, and they are sharing, caring, and protective of one another. Each looks out for the other, and one is always quick to bail the other out of a tight spot. One time their parents forgot to give them money to put in the collection plate at Sunday school. They fumbled around in their pockets and found nothing. Then Tiffie remembered she had a purse with her that had money in it from her recent birthday.

The two sisters had four bills to share. Tiffie took the twenty and the one and gave the ten and the five to Sandie. That Sunday, the children's class had one big offering.

He heals the brokenhearted,
and binds up their wounds.

PSALM 147:3 NRSV

Two minds trading thoughts cause each mind to grow stronger.

ANNA LEE WALDO

I am blue; you are yellow.
Together we make green,
and green is my favorite color.

AUTHOR UNKNOWN

A sister is a gift to the heart, a friend to the
spirit, a gold thread to the meaning of life.

ISADORA JAMES

*Few people are successful
unless a lot of other people
want them to be.*

CHARLIE BROWER

I pray that all may go well with you and
that you may be in good health,
just as it is well with your soul.

3 JOHN 2 NRSV

An older sister helps one remain half-child, half-woman.

AUTHOR UNKNOWN

A sibling may be the keeper of one's identity, the only person with the keys to one's unfettered, more fundamental self.

MARIAN SANDMAIER

One Sister Remembers...

I grew up on a farm with my sister, younger by three years. She and I could get in the biggest messes. One time we discovered a big ball of twine in the hay baler and proceeded to pull it out of the top of the holder and make a great pile on the ground. Then we wrapped the twine around each other and laughed until we thought we'd burst. When we tried to put the twine back in the holder, it wouldn't go. We pushed and threaded but nothing worked, so we hid the ball of twine under the floorboard of Daddy's tractor.

My sister and I have told that story forty years, and it's funnier every time.

Between sisters, often, the child's cry never dies down. "Never leave me," it says; "do not abandon me."

LOUISE BERNIKOW

This is the day which the LORD has made; let us rejoice and be glad in it.

PSALM 118:24 NASB

*We know one another's
faults, virtues, catastrophes,
mortifications, triumphs,
rivalries, desires, and how
long we can each hang by
our hands to a bar. We have
been banded together by pack
codes and tribal laws.*

ROSE MACAULAY

Siblings are the people who teach us about fairness and cooperation and kindness and caring—quite often the hard way.

Pamela Dugdale

Sisters may share the same mother and father but appear to come from different families.

Author Unknown

*Live in harmony with
one another.*

Romans 12:16 NRSV

*We acquire friends and
we make enemies,
but our sisters come
with the territory.*

EVELYN LOEB

God is our shelter and strength,
always ready to help in times of trouble.

PSALM 46:1 GNT

GOD *makes his people strong.*
GOD *gives his people peace.*

PSALM 29:11 THE MESSAGE

You keep your past by having sisters.

DEBORAH MOGGACH

How good it is to have a sister whose heart is as young as your own.

PAM BROWN

Did You Know?

*D*id you know that the famous Brontë sisters initially used other names when they wrote because it was considered unseemly at that time for women to write and publish books? Emily wrote under the name of Ellis Bell, Charlotte wrote as Currer Bell, and Anne called herself Acton Bell. All brilliant writers, they were daughters of a Yorkshire minister. They were close in age and, no matter what they were called, sisters in all things.

God will fully satisfy every need
of yours according to his riches
in glory in Christ Jesus.

PHILIPPIANS 4:19 NRSV

*The happiest people seem
to be those who have no
particular cause for being
happy except that they are so.*

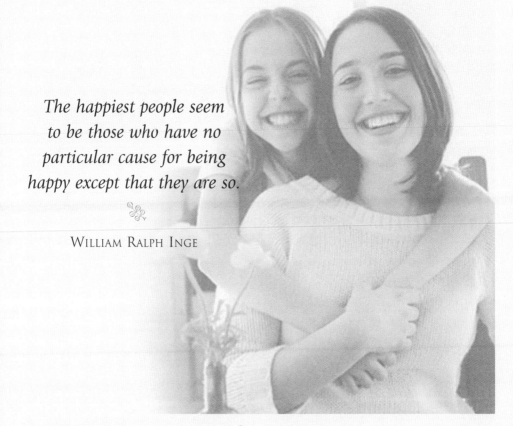

WILLIAM RALPH INGE

The Hebrew word translated "to understand" also means "to listen."

Harold Sala

One of the best ways to persuade others is with your ears—by listening.

Dean Rusk

*Of two sisters one is always the
watcher, the other the dancer.*

Louise Gluck

She is your mirror, shining back at you with a world of possibilities. She is your witness, who sees you at your worst and best, and loves you anyway. She is your partner in crime, your midnight companion, someone who knows when you are smiling, even in the dark. She is your teacher, your defense attorney, your personal press agent, even your shrink. Some days, she's the reason you wish you were an only child.

BARBARA ALPERT

You can't love someone you don't listen to.

MORTON KELSEY

*In order to understand we need to
listen long and attentively.*

PAUL TOURNIER

The desire to be and have a sister is a primitive and profound one that may have everything or nothing to do with the family a woman is born to. It is a desire to know and be known by someone who shares blood and body, history and dreams.

ELIZABETH FISHEL

Survival Tips

*W*ords About Forgiveness:

1. Patience is the source of forgiveness.

2. Love is the heart of forgiveness.

3. Sometimes you need to forgive yourself.

4. God is always willing to forgive.

5. Forgiveness is love in action.

6. Forgiveness opens the future.

7. Forgiveness reunites, reconciles, and restores.

8. Forgiveness is a delete key.

Do not be discouraged, for the LORD your God will be with you wherever you go.

JOSHUA 1:9 NIV

*My sisters have taught
me how to live.*

GEORGE WASSERSTEIN

*Having a sister is like having a best
friend you can't get rid of.*

AMY LI

*An optimist and a pessimist are right
about the same number of times,
but the optimist has more fun.*

WILL ROGERS

*Sisters are for sharing
laughter and wiping tears.*

AUTHOR UNKNOWN